Domain

Domain

Meghan Maguire Dahn

Winner of the 2020 Burnside Review Press Book Award
Selected by Jennifer Chang

Burnside Review Press   Portland, Oregon

Domain
© 2022 Meghan Maguire Dahn

Cover Image: *A Hare in the Forest*, Hans Hoffmann (c. 1585).
Digital image courtesy of the
Getty's Open Content Program.

Cover Design: Susie Steele
Layout: Zach Grow

Printed in the U.S.A.
First Edition, 2022
ISBN: 978-0-9992649-8-0

Burnside Review Press
Portland, Oregon
www.burnsidereview.org

Burnside Review Press titles are available for purchase from the
publisher and Small Press Distribution (www.spdbooks.org).

for my parents, who made a world for me

III. Constraint

FACING THE WATER

Despite the thousand
thousand bodies facing east,
despite the hymnal and restraint
of the group's movements,
despite the ankles in the sand,
despite the answers
rote as gesture on the smallest of us,
despite the vigorous wall of right living
and sound, there was revealed to us
no clear sign.

To sing you cannot keep
your modesty—muscular lift and lilt,
synchronized breath, organ on organ.
No ornament, no coupling.
You take the waters.
You take the unreliable wind.
You consign yourself
to your own uncertain cells.

What can't the ribs forgive.
Grit of first thought: no
sound is incomplete.

I. Cultivation

I will sit right down
waiting for the gift of sound
and vision.

—David Bowie

What if the expected calm were rotten,
after all. Where would I be then? Pink

in the symptoms of shock, rising
to your cotton, your sedative glove.

You pull the gauze from my pulse,
redeem the pulp of it alone. And if

you said now, *unknot this used up breast—*
what municipality would be mine,

what abandoned cell.

THE OTHER TRODDEN IN CLOVER AND TIMOTHY
after Carolina Ebeid

At the center of my trust, a lamb is leaning
warm with worry. There, too, is its weaning.

My daughter tells me when you fall asleep
that's all your sin falling off. I cannot change

the impulses of others, nor can I change
what solace violence can bring. Every flock

establishes an economy, a geometric field
of survival. I read recently of selfish herd theory—

the repeated movement of individuals to the center,
forcing, again and again, their neighbors

into the peril of the periphery. The quickest,
the strongest, the most dominant ones

avoid predation in this way. I am not your best
beast of perpetual motion. Tell me an act

is an act and not something greater, and I bleat
an angry answer, sodden with the belief

that acts signify. In the teeth of the wolf—*look*—
there is the fleece of the lamb the ewe pushed out.

TO SHRIKE

If you ask me to be
I am always hungry for the spindle.

Savage bird, and small,

I am your bread and butter,

your mammal, your anything
with fur. I was self-satisfied.

I was smug in the sweet rot—
even happy, even poor, even
stubborn in my mornings.

My kind can hollow a whole hill. Gnaw
our teeth right in the jaw.

Your own bones take no practice at all.

If I wanted to be
symbolic about it, I'd beg
for the barb of a yew.

We both know I'm game for any sharp thing

when you lift me up.

I am the warped thing that wanted never.

      I would watch
and I would be watched.

      I would measure
and I would take the rod.

Even 224km skyward I am
everyone's almost-sated fantasy.

Febrile mirror—

the true position of ecstasy
is the stasis-

posture of supermodels.

I am about to begin my fiery fall.

              Naked pull
of gravity—my more perfect knowing

of how the oceans move.

Toward What Abyss

The FAA has identified 482 bird species that were hit in the U.S. from
1990 through 2012. Airplanes run into loons, starlings, grebes, pelicans,
cormorants, herons, storks, egrets, swans, ducks, vultures, hawks, eagles,
cranes, sandpipers, gulls, pigeons, cuckoos, owls, turkeys, blackbirds, crows,
chickadees, woodpeckers, hummingbirds, mockingbirds, parrots, bats—as
well as various kinds of geese. —Eric Uhlfelder, for *National Geographic*

They carry the oil to the field in jugs. They set to the slick work.
This municipal labor—anointing eggs, clearing skies—

it is like I said: to exterminate is a kind of knowing
and it doesn't come cheap. Terrible cargo, otherworldly chick.

It's called a bird strike, this collision, when it occurs. After,
there is a man who swabs the blood and feather and bone

from the plane. He sends the swab to a woman named Dove
who knows every node and microstructure, every sequence of DNA.

From her office, she creates accordances—the remains of birds
to the Consortium for the Barcode of Life. She reports

to the BASH (Bird/Wildlife Aircraft Strike Hazard)
and BAM (Bird Avoidance Model) initiatives. A spool of thread

subject to the laws of physics cannot save us
from all our fears. Come, doctor—organize our flight.

Public Works

On the first day the pale blood,
the signal fire.
The next day giant snails

descend on Florida to mate
by the thousands.
If you have ever seen them at it,

the iridescent twist and release,
you won't wonder
that they're drawn to me.

On the third day we must ask
what matters more—
Beauty or the Public Good.

I say let the world glisten in
the aftersex
of snails. If you break your neck

I'll heal you
and each of your subordinates
slowly in my lap.

Outside, the impatience and pleading
of the neighborhood traffic is transparent
to the backlit view. I want to gather

the best, right angle of day
and all the wistful revving of every engine
primed to show the world

what's what. Which undergarments
are most architectural in their yearnings,
which bulbs most assertive under

the superintendent's hands. Jesus,
that soil is black and my fingers are clean
and if you think I'm as good

as the bartender's house tab, as orderly
as his shift splits, I want you to know
my equipment is porcelain and my intentions

are beginning to sleep.

I asked the broker *Where is want*
and she took me to the trees
I could afford: Tree of Heaven,
tree of invasion, tree of filling space.

New York has a million
hungers working like gravities.
Say you disembark, a mosaic of light
grabs at your fractured self—
your arm, your knee—and says (oh,
jealousy) *At long last*. At my back

a widow waits a decade. Yearly, she lays out
the grief, the gun, the locks,
the candles, the cuffs and calls
to her husband *You must answer*
to get help. From an empty place
our hands touch an empty sign.

                    It says *Take*
One. Oh please, put your hands on
any none. A hundred years ago the mastodon
lay still under Inwood. Now every last looted
tooth is returned to the museum, that lockbox
of the untouchable touched.

At the start, when we first talked of nightfall,
we meant that on the land
a physical darkness physically fell.
Want is in the fall risk and I want it
in my hands.

TONGUE OF THE DOCTOR, TONGUE OF THE DOG
after Stephen Crane

You followed the satin ribbon,
the detritus, the jealous feeling in the forest
to the suicide, who, among the drying mulberries,
allowed a pup to lick her wound.
"It is sovereign and clear," she said, "and here
is my certificate." She pulled it
from a knot in her gut. You tried
to write her a letter on the spot.
You tried to look her in the eyes.
There are things you cannot do
in the forest. You said, "Stay.
Please, sit." You touched behind her ears.
"It is good. It is good."

Into an era, an apple or an orchard
of decisions. Tradition thrives on practice.
The wealthy are buying up the ranches.

On the pleasant days—sky impossible,
breeze low—the farmers downhill work
their culverts, chest high in a ditch,

digging against what water will come.
A mule. A mean dog. At a meeting,
an old man starts to quote the chapter

and line of the land grant. Not the Bible.
Not the letter from his son. (Honey in the mouth,
bile in the hands.) Beautiful

as a roadside memorial adorned
in tinsel and shamrocks. Any holy day will do.
The whole world wicks the water

right out of you and into itself. The bus stops
are blue and unattended by patron or transport.
You step over a dead cat, its rigid tongue.

The plague thrives here. (Honey in the soul,
bile in the skin.) The buzzards are immune,
but you are not. Do not bury the cat.

Improbable tinder of syringes—orange
and discarded. Tin foil. Candy wrappers.
All of it looking like so many rosaries tangled

in cottonwood. (Honey in the mind,
bile in the vein.) Be thou opened,
be thou left unalone by the dead.

to stop the savage dogs
to cut away the old growth
to forge a painless birth
to warn outsiders they are welcome to the tooth
to abandon the spirit
to slice bread or your throat
to make a cradle safe
to keep the warrior, buried
to obstruct nightmare
to sever friendship, or, if not—to trade for dove or coin
to imitate white mica glinting in red hills
to imitate your teeth grinning in your red mouth
to determine the best course of action with a blind throw
        (right is with the lord, left and someone's done for)
to revere the first tool, the flint blade
to mark the way of he who follows the sun, to skin
        the moon (your hard work is for nothing)
to draw magnets from the ground below
to call forth the flood

QUESTION

You will walk the stonewall of my heart
uncannily. They use mortar here

so you think it's normal
not to cut a stone, not to find

its friction complete in the stack.
I want you to know all my good intentions

boil over when I think you don't leave
me in my natural state, but in a state

suspended by imperfect choices. We could
carve our outlines where we land,

but you can't tell me I wasn't beatific
when I pushed the stones together all afternoon

in the woods.

Self Portrait with Lacrimae Rerum and Eyelid Pulled Down

My face has made offerings
to the weather all winter. Integration
waits for me out the door and objects
dolorous in their daytime pace
find their way to me.
The tears of things
take place at every moment, stalking
a mortal mind and its touch.
I want to be touched by the stutter-green
sorrow of our whole world and every augury
no one ever taught me. And so, eyelid
pulled down half the time, I watch
for all the birds I should never include
in a poem. In their speed
they have outpaced my hope
as when I let a woman lean against me
on the Bx7. She trembles when she yells
at her man to stop crying to her
about the chances she won't keep giving.

Summer of getting trashed in the woods
Summer of viscous approach to any problem
Summer of Luna Moth at my gate
Summer of my own damn money

> What did the summer carry in itself?
> *A ransom of feathers that hold*
> *the sum of the day's light toothed*
> *in place and fully contemplated.*

Summer of the belief in my general unimpregnability
Summer of perfect values
Summer of attempted rape on the lawn of someone's out-of-town parents
Summer of being saved (Mount Hope River, brindled light)

> What are the means of ingress?
> *In equal shares: alcohol, bitterness, beauty.*
> *Put a razor under your tongue and climb the cliff face.*

Summer of teaching a boy to take fluids
Summer of Billy running from his ghost, bottle in hand
Summer of running my feet bloody/Summer of eating again
Summer of know your place, bitch

> If you were to remove it, what would be the shape of its lack?
> *The shape of the lack would take one of two forms—*
> *the flame or the rose. But hush.*

Summer of keep your head down
Summer of honest work
Summer of Ryan falling eight stories onto concrete

Summer he was John Doe

> What would your mother say?
> *My mother would, and did, say I am as a migratory creature*
> *and she is my oyamel fir. My mother, found by magnet and riverbed.*

Summer of being told I know a lot about love
Summer of petulant goodbyes
Summer of contraband (Pakistani boot knife, eagle feather, machete)
Summer of short hems

> When summer pinches you by the Achilles and dips you in,
> do you submit?
> *To do so means you accept the inevitability of your own death.*

Summer of AM broadcasts and peepers
Summer of bad advice
Summer of busted knuckles
Summer of cherry red

> What is the essence and what does it reveal to you?
> *When you hike it up, you will see your inner rope,*
> *you will see it all work out.*

HEAVEN'S GATE

It was my year under the comet.
Hale-Bopp: twin-tailed and increasing.

Plants started to die.
Even the inattentive felt the inaccuracy

of the network news.
There was never any knowing.

There was never any ascent of the ladder.

In the spading under, my hands
got dirty. *Soil, nettle, plum, and fern.*

It was my year to feel most at odds—

this husk would buck and jolt
in its own time until I did my work,

sequestered all the light into a small fold
of mind, continued whatever task was at hand:

kissing, parking the car.

Apple, mulch, pup, little plover, little pebble.
Nothing easier.

Cohesion took a fortnight, took a season.

39 people died under purple silk.
They wore their new Nikes.

Do and Ti, a full scale. A son-mother,
a father-wife. A note knotted back and dissonant.

I stayed behind in the bend.

I could put my hand on any tree.

There are many reasons I cannot sleep—
among them, the percussion of what I can do
versus what I cannot. I have been breaking pecans,

magnificently, all week. I have been enamored
with the most shallow of thoughts. I have remained
unaware of the housefly and the gnat, hungry

and approaching my left side. My instructor suggests
I try to breathe through my eyes only, knowing
their permeability. I begin to consider my eyes the best

nesting place for the insects I have captivated.
I waiver when I value the goodness of the world
to be less than my own failures. No one has spoken

to me of the hidden things! I break my own heart
and reparations, when I make them, will disappoint.
If my failings involve trapping moths under the eaves

on my way to bed, rather than some machination
of my own contrivance, what I mean is I have done
disservice to the dignity of love. This morning

I swatted at a beetle merely because I had grown tired
of watching its progress across my thigh.
I redouble my efforts at basic moral acceptability.

> Right now I am looking and I swear to you
> the river is pink.

NEVER AND BEAST

In the darker months I made my bed
and Never, who left me fumbling and dumb,
courted a pulse faster and faster.
          Future purpose: let me burrow and settle
in a river that is also silt—
all my shortcomings are brown and slick,
wet home to my own hibernation.
Hushed fact of me in a riverbed!

You did so show your teeth.
I became all soft belly and long neck.
A thing to bite upon and the ground
into which it retreats.

With Never let me divide
time from its purpose;
if I pull my breath from yours,
isolation will open an unlatched aperture in me:

River and cold blood,
weasel and pelt.

I am on edge—my vision improves with the heat.
When I faint my neck is livid.
Father and I paint the oak stump thick with tar.

      / /

The light that insists on my skin
is stubborn in the tar pits—the gasoline
creeks along the fault line.

      / /

I failed to excavate the excellent mammoth.
I hear the flies anoint the pit. Graceful,
for once, I entice one to my eyelid.

The earthworm pets are yours for a day.
Having loved, you are mud.

You are the unsounded sound
that I hear in my too-thick bones.

You are will of the wisp. You are liable
to swoon and to doodle, to sketch the line of future names.

Make your aim blue, your brown-eyed faces
true to purpose. Be blind to gesture.

Here is the window of sight: plaster it.
Here is the window of taste: plaster it.

Here is the window of scent: fill it with straw and cover it with mud.
Here is the window of flesh: submerge it in the mud.

Here is the window of sound: seal it with mud.
You are the hidden and the mud.

II. Clarity

Also in this He shewed a littil thing the quantitye of an hesil nutt in the palme of my hand, and it was as round as a balle. I lokid there upon with eye of my understondyng and thowte, What may this be?

—Julian of Norwich

THE CONDITIONS OF CLARITY

I slip very quietly into the water—if it's appropriate.
I could never make all the sounds—flooded sinus

as acoustic fat, clavicle as strap tooth. The wake
I make on my mother's life is the best right whale.

You can tell me the rain is blinding. If I say
the water is limpid it is. I will never be the scientist

naked in your environment; I don't engender sympathy
in the cold salt water of another. But I know a clarity

that rises from toe to crown, so I'm no philanthropist
for your skeleton and its shadows.

(Mysterious and Subtle Mirror!)

I keep this cloud in my mouth
and only let it out
on occasions of true contrition.

If you rub two things together long enough
they will both bruise. That is how you know
contrition and time and my cloud.

Darling, on this planet of distance
there is little I regret, but I promise you—
I am still waiting for the bruise:

I am still approaching my own cloud
knowing how quickly it can disperse.
I promise you one day the cloud will cover us

and everything we forgot will walk
shoulder to shoulder with us
until we recover all that completeness.

There is a remedy for regret: ask me
into the bathroom. I will breathe onto the mirror
until we are both gone

and though we know this blindness
can't last, in that moment we'll admit grace
through our useless eyes.

Opacity—O cloud—
what life is there for an abyss in a body?
What loneliness behind my lips.

A River Is a Sweet-Talker Anyway,

                                        and the ear
is prone to drowsiness at mid-day and at evening. When a queen confesses

the whole world wants a piece. You too.

I am merely me, my habits.
When I was nine I thought I could save the whole world:

if I circled a tree three times
my father would come home safe; if I delivered
the sequence of names to the night sky

everyone would live till morning.

St. John Nepomuk drowned floating
under five stars, having kept
his mouth shut. He did not sink.

I haven't forgotten how to do litany:
looking at Cassiopeia through binoculars

(borrowed), time crossing its hooves,
I keep my secrets. I say my prayers.
They are so many milagros, perfectly stacked

and in unflinching order.

RIVER

Gravity set you down like the bad silverware,
                skinned your shoulders. Your snare
released   the particulars.

Our yelps awakened   the old tapestry
                of your flesh.
                We ran to you blankly.

You're no more
than the bulk grain that bends the back
            at the burrow's flank.

All morning your nothingness
kept clanging at the halls.   We attended
the river eroding our wishes for you.

        You twist   lamb-lithe, sopping
in your loud plaid.
Your eyes close quick.   The square of your mouth

   coughs up its brilliant confession:
I have not worked grief.
I have not stopped the flow of water.

SOME BEES LIVE THEIR WHOLE LIVES CLEANING THE LEGS OF FORAGERS

In the rafters, a language of flight—
call it a swarm—opened itself
above you. You had found me

in the cathedral of another, wanting
to chart an approach;

my hands hummed
over an imagined topography.

*

Some bees read flowers.

Liars are nothing to them. A tulip,
for instance, will broadcast a false bounty
when everyone knows it's already been opened up.

Watch out for that tulip, they say.
They gossip all day. They know each other
as themselves, tangled in phone cords.

*

When you found me in that wrong geography
I was trying to behave myself, I was trying
on every Right Idea. This work
aggravates me. I play my options
like a piano with missing keys, arpeggios useless,
fingers stubbed on dumb notes. You took
my hands in yours (I haven't forgotten) and made me a promise

No one's going to drown you in rose petals
for being uncouth at dinner, Meghan.

*

We build our language like a map
of electromagnetic fields.
The sundry signal hairs worry
a dictionary across our backs,
the book of everything we've fallen for,
all the pollen from our knees.

*

The swarm was singing
loud as high tension lines
above us. Each measure
is enough to repeat.

Won't we shake
when we find each other?
Won't we work for the fall, fill
each cell with what's golden,
an accretion of what we've known
of truth, of the Great Afterall.

CALVE

Let me tell you, there is one thing left
to build—and this is how it always is, measured
down to the cubic centimeter. What I mean

is limits. The edge of a cloud, for instance,
collides with dry air and you'd think
the encounter would be a slow work,

a dissipation, but it is exactly always instant—
evaporation, entire or in part. What remains
of cloud is cloud.

Try to reduce it more—you can fly a drone
into the throat of a glacial sinkhole
just like they did on the news

and if you think it's easy to distinguish
water lubricating ice from ice, headlines
from your own handsome panic, well

think of where you came from
and what you have left to build.

Of the Hermit Bent Double by His Chains and His Follower

It being the only way, I will
lay myself at your feet
that you may look
me in the eye when I pray
for you. Of my lesser hungers
I admit openly your disgust.
Of my keening I'll allow
your claim: luxury. Little
clockwork, helpful hinge—
When you're in heaven won't you
laugh and laugh? As I am now
so I shall be world without
letting go. Your acolyte
licking up the dust your lashes
leave behind.

THE FIRST GILT

On December 31, 2013, China's HD satellite Gaofen-1 opened its eyes.

Anointed with the gold of the opulent eyes,
this year's new island, this year's worst
earthquake are awake to the infant, its soft

technology. From any house, bones down
in winter, cobwebs or not, it can direct
its eyes to the bend of day, see the turn

of painted change. Dilation is dirty work.
Any opening invites the wanted and unwanted—
rice and smog, calamities and capabilities.

No more precision agriculture, no more city planning,
no more bicycles. When we are beheld we lose a membrane
to the open maw of the eye. We peel off and off.

It gobbles us up. The infant ate whole
a suspension bridge. It ate a thrush and a chestnut.
It ate the golden suckling pig

with all her offspring—preposterous
and prosperous on a Chinese wedding collar.
In the new year, the hungry satellite transmits:

every sight a school choir.

Instructions for Blinking
after Julio Cortázar

The ancient Romans believed that objects emitted a transparent film or *simulacrum* that would float off of an object and into the eye of the beholder whenever it was gazed upon. While it is unclear what happened to these simulacra when an object was not being gazed upon, it should be self-evident that it is in your best interest to believe that this is the way of the physical world today, even with all of the advances in science.

Deep in the recesses of your eyes reside small magnets. These are the same ones that turn your head on its axis when your beloved walks by or when an embarrassingly rich example of unhinged dancing occurs in your vicinity on a late night subway platform. The magnets attract the simulacra, inviting them in. When your mother was the maddest at you that she had ever been she said, "Get out of my sight—I can't stand to look at you right now." It is because she didn't want her eyes to absorb a little folded up version of naughty, naughty you.

Blinking is the filing system for simulacra. In order to avoid a congestion of the eyes it is important to blink at an average frequency of 17/minute, or 26/minute if you're under emotional duress. You may think that blinking is a fully involuntary action. It is not. You must first weight the top lid by imagining a regret. The size of the regret and subject of it will determine the basic forcefulness of the resulting blink. Next, encourage buoyancy in your bottom lid. It's best to picture a cloud or cherry blossom for a moment to achieve this.

The resulting blink, of course, should be of short duration. No need to make people stare or to appear as though you're in a rapturous state.

When you open your eyes again you should feel relief. If not, an aggravation has occurred and you must renew the process immediately with purer intent.

During the Meteor Shower

The last time I saw him
he was breaking down my door,
he was burning apart
in the upper atmosphere.

I am easy to bruise
for something so fearsome.
I will come apart underground.

That year, I wore my hair so long
I could thread a needle,
make embroidery
of the clover, its roots.

TAME WILLOW AND THE UNBELIEVERS
for Herr Otto Edler von Graeve, wuenschelrutenforscher

In your West, I am porous.
My every fiber bows
when I am fine and subtle
in my approach.

> I willow grip left
> and lay knuckles
> right. Resting,

my pulse is 75 without exception.
Reliable old chum. Susceptible,
though, to springs, to radium,
to the smallest rope of gold.

I am a kind conduit. I am my pulse
under the influence of your future
markets, your nest egg, the estate
of your great grandchildren.

> Take my silver thread
> and feel it thrill.
> *You have no skill and I have much.*

Fear not for the hidden things:
a rabbit warren, a well undrilled, a ledge you cannot see.
These will oblige you on your sick bed.

Give me all your doubt to ferry.
I am no professor, but I've got
my leather, my register, the bit of felt at my waist.

VISCOSITY

Glassy eel of doubt, in the morning
I did too little, unaccustomed to exposure

as a means of preservation. When I took you
in my hands I tore you up and lost my hope.

Eel of doubt at midday, when you made
your way through wet grass I laughed

for you and you wrapped your ventricle vein
around me. I began to suspect

my island was a place to build a life
for us, without trains or commerce.

Only barges ever passed by us
bearing winter's salt in mountains and in heaps.

Silver eel of evening, by the glaucous hour
I had reversed my stance. The water and the sky

took prominence and my footing
was on nothing in between. My patience

had grown bare. When I looked at the houses
across the bank, I saw them swelter in their goodness.

I know how I must look to you.
If you suggest I've made the bed wrong

I'll believe you. I'll go for a walk,

welcome the affection of the neighbor's cat.

When I make the map of us, my long doubt,
I will lay you down feldgrau, without water,

use you as my scale. For someone who knows
what's right, I have a lot of trouble

acting decently without distance.

GENUFLECTION

I am always trying to have polite conversation
with my own guilt: rose tea with juniper berry.

Bitterness abrades a delicate thing. Blundering
old bully. Marmoreal hypocrite. I am unrelenting

even in the presence of my strong little girls. Oh,
you skinned knees of the world, I promise you—

who climb any tree at all, delighted by capability—
I want to be kind when exposed. I knock back

my potential for invisibility. Any day now
I will be bridled in a stampede, pressed close

by the bison as they abandon the valley. I will go along:
I am always looking to be deconsecrated by nature.

Nobody wishes for boredom, debt. I begin to suspect
there is no appropriate ointment. To taste

a little of a poison thing is to reflect. Put down
the Tiger Balm. I will give up my perfect height.

Self, oh Self, how you felt it when you stepped
to the cormorant with the cloud you wanted

to represent your shame and it called to you *Who robs,*
who robs for you all. The cold illegibility set in.

You watched your other hand insert the lancet.
Who can know the shrill truth of Meaning

when the elements have run amok. So,
you returned to the cormorant

with the cloud you intended to represent
all your culpability, smug in a tin cup.

When the bird started in again
you battered the cup with a star, let it hang

from her beak. Enough talk, oh
Self, ah Soul, of oil spills.

               Are you listening
to the rust, the justified sinner, the simpletons?

Some people need the lesson of the-world-will-not-
fall-apart. Over and over, all day

it is important to consider quiddity— you
have made an ordered flower of it.

When you are given the chance to return,
to name everything you know, try to hold things soft

in the cage of your throat. Do not try to get it right.

III. Constraint

I would bind narcissus to narcissus.

—H. D.

THE CONDITIONS OF CONSTRAINT
after G. M. Hopkins

If in a forest—rude, pregnant, wet—
your eyes exhaust themselves

> and eleven birds—all unruly,
> > syntactic, quick—select a strand
> > of your cooperative hair
>
> and ingenuity (bickering to the hilt,
> > allowing the future form) gives rise to a nest
> > knotting itself under the air
>
> and the things you used for motifs
> > were not pretty or headstrong,
> > but downright pig-headed (like the electric bill
> > or the font you hung—*holy, o particular*
> > *purity*—in the mudroom)
>
> and those grave distractions—the hungers,
> > all the sublime joys—open in you like a book,

then let the thrall of changing cells take you,
your corporation of proteins, your rhetoric unspooled.

Never Do Housework with Imperfect Intent

When I was a housewife
I was the finest egret.
I would wait all day

for any train—yours
or any of a hundred commuters'
as they flit their course on Narragansett.

I'd wade the anticonvulsant radius,
free of rope and sympathy.
We made a runt. Our glass half

empty. On the heirloom Blue Willow
I painted a beast. Each on each.
The withering work. My form

had been perfect. Now I cover
the mirrors. To approach god
build a charge with every coiling,

every uncoiling atom. *Left left left.*
Heart heart heart. I will chew
this secret when it grows full.

I will fold small clothes with my beak.

1. One Hand Receiving, the Other Guarding the Knee

    Gravity, always plump under the atmosphere, welcomes a small cup.
    My hand is always small. My knee is warm enough.

2. Pinching in a Passive Fashion

    as you would a butterfly or heirloom lace
    as you would the earlobe of a sleeping child

3. Elegantly Draped Ring Finger on Otherwise Nonchalant Hand

    I was the aristocrat's first daughter:
    when I pumped water from the well, I did so with grace.

4. Left Hand Receptive to the Northern Water Snake

    Where I am from the best prayer is a flexible spine.

5. Hands Perched as though above Tangerines

    The egg timer is a holy thing,
    the bell—a small crisis.

6. Two Clenched Fists

    in the folds of an opera cape

7. Holding an Absent Object in the One Remaining Hand

    Empty out your devotion: this is the only reasonable approach
    to the path between made and unmade.

8. Hand Cascading, as if to Feed Lion

    To eat a small thing is to submit entirely to time.

Samo for the So-Called Avant Garde

Make me bend the knee, crown to ground,

Architect, Man of the Sun. I will never question
your long-shot guess, nor your name-dropping.

I'll watch your skin shine, your fist full of ash.

Spar with me anytime.
I've got your telegrams in pocket—

I've got your $2,000. We'll stop at lunchtime

to eat the last of your shame and send those Philistines
postcards of my legs and all my condensed histories

in a pile on the bed—*all those little mental icons of the time...*

I can be ugly. I can take a pounding. Submit me
to fire and I will still be your tin girl, not your gold.

I copy your dreams to drawings—three hundred foxes
aflame, the fields a wreck, and your blind heroism.

I do not have a name for that which consumes the day,

the cacophony of your bright hair.

But I can pack a valise full of asbestos. My lungs
will suffer the sequester, the weaving,

the production of your shroud.

You will not withstand the flames.
But your shroud will remain for a little gold frame,

a little fame in the halls of our great museums.

ASK

Die for it. Isn't it pretty? —Lou Reed

I will hold a perfect pearl inasmuch as every pearl is perfect,
inasmuch as I don't mean plastic on a string. I will not drop it.
I will not plant it in the ground. No amount of rain

will stop my sweet talk or my counting. To count is to substitute
a thing for a progression—your followers, the fanatical sunflowers.
I will count every man entering the dollar store.

A fan's a two-faced, worrisome thing: he is a necessary receptacle
and a person who would dissolve talent beneath his tongue.
I am not looking for a moon face any day; I am holding my pearl.

I am dosing my math. Where one requires cohesion, two needs
abrasion, three: calcification. Four is an earthly thing.
Five is an eternity. There are not many men who shop the wife aisle

pushing an overfull cart with votives and off-season wrapping paper,
baby wipes and multi-purpose cleaner. Orpheus
needed a perfect fan, not a companion for one or any number of nights.

I would not die for a train whistle. I would not die for a lie.
I would die for a tree crying under ice. When I know
things are wrong, I am right to cry or to grasp at items

other people set down to purchase. I am right to incur the aggravation
of the cashier, to provoke her nacre. Wouldn't I die
for something pretty. Wouldn't I make myself a pearl.

That fall no one in town
could make sense of distances.
All our horses dove the rivers—

carts over bridges, even the backyard
ponies ran amok. Cry for them.
Too confused to open

his cache of quicksilver,
the dentist reached
for his vacation jade,

filled our mouths like emperors.
A bobcat saved a fledgling.
A grown man

cried when—unable to discern
an apple from the blood moon—
he harvested all our hope,

ruined the careful chart of the tides,
ended entire generations
for the sake of his own hunger.

It all started when I lied and, slowly,
as I copied out my punishment
(the Stoics—first in Greek, then English),

things aligned to themselves.
"Virtue is a craft." (Good craft, keep me.)
Somewhere above me, 200 miles

skyward, a woman is a levity
of hair and necklace and thread, quilting
in the International Space Station.

I, at least, have moved horses to water
and back to dry land. If I move
my precious mouth, let it be for keeping time,

let it be for the right living of all beasts.

To the Extent That I Am, I Am Alone All Night

There is little to separate me from the wolfdog
howling behind the straw-bale wall.

He's got the coyotes going again.
Everyone here has mutts—not for love,

but for aggression. I cannot make it sweet
or supple. Outside, I have nothing to do.

I accustom myself to 125 pounds
of muscle and bite trying to level

the fence as I pass. The girls are calling
on a bad line. They can't hear me.

So loudly do they call they've set the mutts
for blood, the wolfdog carving glyphs

in the adobe. The ranchers used barbed wire
to pirate a telephone network.

Who talks to outsiders, anyway? When I walk
the teenagers are raising dust with diesel.

They wear masks. They want to take me on.
I don't look like anyone. Even the light off a flagstone

singes me. At 8,000 feet I feel every step.
I am not welcome on ranch roads,

in cemeteries. I am allowed to a thousand

horses running the four directions, though,

converging on the spot in the arroyo
where a cross keeps returning.

You cannot glean an old song for your own
without making some kind of payment.

If I lay down for it, a man will recite his dream
and I will take the hoof.

MY THROAT INCARNATE

I've perched on the rim
of my parents' well—

rock hammered into water.
It sounded

like our killing parts
made metronomic.

I will match anyone hot
breath for hot breath.

See who gets the kill. Flex,
tear-and-gnash, delight—all of it:

flinch lip, arch
tongue to palate,

hitch eyes back
to pineal gland.

The garter snake
in the goldenrod—

I held its excised heart.
It beat in my palm.

MATTHEW

In the thicket we made
        of hammered gold
we face each other, flowers

        almost in our glad teeth.
Our chains are silver and grateful
        at the fetlocks. We yell

with our four plump lungs
        our lazuli of gratitudes;
we whinny our discontents,

        a game with bad rules.
Every gold leaf is burnished
        to blear on the pitch of us.

That time I took you to the river
        and you put every part of you
in it I thought *paradise*, I thought

        joy. If there were ever another
moment, it is always the next
        now, this verdigris composing

our faces.

A NAME

I do not know how to call
        shrouded in uncertainty,
                To the extent I can allow that
it existed,   names apart
    tiny-little, maybebaby, salamander.

I tried once   swallowed me,
and once for
        its father.   an honor

    Repetitions sloughed off and hitches in time.

 had to use tampons   . My blood hummed.
                in the trash, I tried
to construct an apology.
        modify the offending behavior
and I kept bleeding

       space between my body
and something   .   space was too small to hear.
   inept and illiterate and I could not hear
the space   . Not some blooming
cabbage, but blood and pain and cells organized

into I know not what. And then into the trash.
The right thing   spade
to earth and bury them there. The right thing

Spade to earth and bury me there, too.

Under a rock, in the woods.

A BARTER

The white slug of my first promise

makes work of the field mice.   Silvers them
in the woods; and—well, you can always bury
them with the ferns if you want.

Propagate more ferns.

My first time: I was five,   still
young enough my mother came to me
her face not taut, I rocked her,

volunteered *I promise*   *I promise my promise*.

My reconstitution to the green lion
and my subsequent attempts to eat the sun, a fool's progress
across my mother's body to

the sour milk of time.

The curdling.

Ever since that day
I told them—*Slugs,
adorn* me *for the ferns*.

SHRIFT

The necessary grace was to slip
my hand in the bucket of warm milk, in the mouth
of the calf who rammed it to bleeding

on the edge of the bucket. What labyrinth
congealed in oak. What thread I lent
to the endeavor. The animal was not mine,

nor would ever be. She was an exhibition:
two barns down, children learned to pull nothing
from nothing beneath a fiberglass model

of a mother. Let me tell you how slight it was:
I forgot myself. I overreached. Scalding
authority—to decide the shape of another.

Kindness, when it comes, is a cord.
When I let it fray, I mustn't despair—there's a manual
for every type of repair. Mostly it calls for gold.

By which I mean: I should give
my blood carefully. I should rest my hand
on the soft places of my growing doubts

just as I would any felt. When I curate
the true things I've touched: every animal
draws crowds. They stare out of my heart

and into the empty space that I obeyed.
I can pile on the words. My mother tells me
when I was a child I would talk and talk

when tired. I would bend my head down
to my knees and swing around, release from harbor
the entire day's thoughts in quick succession.

At my best, I try to believe the air
will lift every subtle fact I've known.
Despite its heft, I want it all to never end.

JUSTIFICATION IN REVERSE

I have been cautious—

      I am able to cradle my own
      hand in my own hand.

Born of uncertain eyesight,

      I was obsessed with blotting paper
      in the warmest, in the greyest hour.

None of my thoughts conclude gracefully.
They peregrinate the inalterable errors, hairline
fissures, desiccated riverbeds

                  all summer, anytime.

I have been instructed in forgiveness:

      I am plumb on the doorframe,
      I am suspicious of the easy hinge.

DENDRITE

It is always October when I allow
a furrow of lightning in. What a fool—
to want everything the skin can know.

A window is the cruelest part
of any house. It tames the whole blue
orchestration of sky. My heart, inert,

wants a little continuity, just enough
to survive the bolt, mind intact,
bones branching with electricity.

I never said it would be easy.
Will I know the noise and gold
of these backbones?

It's not love that calls me out the sill
to where the animals are unafraid.
It is thirst. I would swallow every thought.

I want my place in a snarl of laurels—
neglected, wholesome, and unmade.
Give me my one hour with the immortals.

"Facing the Water": Based on the incredible pamphlets of Ida B. Craddock. She believed it was her calling to teach married people how to love each other physically and was eventually arrested by the Postmaster General for distributing obscene materials through the mail. When she was a child, her religious congregation would wake up and sing facing the ocean together at dawn.

"The Other Trodden in Clover and Timothy": *Worrying* is the name for the physiological response lambs and sheep have to being chased.

"Tongue of the Doctor, Tongue of the Dog": The forest in question is Aokigahara, near Mount Fiji in Japan. Dog saliva has been shown to have antimicrobial and antibacterial properties. So, going off to lick your wounds might not be so bad after all.

"Analgesia": This poem and a number of others in the book are set in Chimayó, New Mexico. Chimayó is known for three things: (1) it's a pilgrimage site with a well of holy dirt, (2) it's the birthplace of the most iconic form of southwestern weaving, and (3) it has a heroin problem.

"A Knife at the Crossroads, Pointing East": Another Chimayó poem. This is about an actual knife that I found at an actual crossroads, actually pointing east. At the heart of this poem is the impossibility of depicting a thing that is already perfectly poetic in reality.

"Self Portrait with Lacrimae Rerum and Eyelid Pulled Down": *Lacrimae Rerum* could either be translated as "tears for things" or "tears of things." I like thinking that it could be both at the same time.

"Heaven's Gate": This poem is set during the year the Heaven's Gate cult committed mass suicide in an attempt to ascend to the Hale-Bopp comet.

"Deprivation": This poem is in widerruf with Thomas James.

"The Conditions of Reason": In his *The Scale of Perfection* Walter Hilton writes of the house of five windows. A thief could come in through any one of them and create ruin.

"(Mysterious and Subtle Mirror!)": The title of this poem comes from an aside in "The Lovers" by the astonishing Silvina Ocampo. The poem is deeply haunted by *The Cloud of Unknowing*.

"River": The *Egyptian Book of the Dead* describes the 42 negative confessions one must perform upon dying. I love the notion that we would spend our first moments not living proving a lack. This poem is in widerruf with Sylvia Plath.

"Some Bees Live Their Whole Lives Cleaning the Legs of Foragers": This poem is for Max Ritvo, who really did make jokes like that about drowning the dinner guests in roses for being uncouth.

"Calve": There is a book that has been a favorite in the Salyer/Dahn household for many years now: Matthea Harvey's *Cecil the Pet Glacier*. This poem is a bit of an answer to that book.

"Of the Hermit Bent Double by His Chains and His Follower": I borrowed a book on St. Jerome (patron saint of translators) from the great Richard Howard. In that book, there was a passage describing the "lesser Stoics" who were hermits during the same time as Jerome. There was one who decided the best way to be a Stoic was to chain his neck to his ankles and live that way, folded in half, for years. Like many people who make a spectacle of their self-imposed suffering, he had very enthusiastic fans. This poem's speaker is one of those fans.

"Tame Willow and the Unbelievers": I'm pretty sure if this poetry thing doesn't work out I'd make a really excellent dowser.

"Viscosity": American eels start their lives transparent and then, as they travel through different environments, gain their color.

"Never Do Housework with Imperfect Intent": This poem takes its notion of atomic prayer, wherein the more we can strip away the trappings of syntax the closer we can get to god, from *The Cloud of Unknowing*.

"Traveling Altar Bearing the Eight Auspicious Gestures": This poem is inspired by the absolutely idiosyncratic collection of the Nicholas Roerich Museum on West 107th Street in New York.

"Samo for the So-Called Avant Garde": Portions of this poem quote postcards by Jean-Michel Basquiat.

"Ask": This poem imagines the great Lou Reed through the lens of the medieval poem *Pearl* by the Gawaine poet.

"Matthew": This poem is, unsurprisingly, for Matthew Carey Salyer. I was imagining the two of us as the figures of the Rams in the Thicket from 2600-2400 BCE, discovered in the Royal Cemetery at Ur. The two rams that would have held a ceremonial vessel no longer face each other, two confronted animals, but are continents apart.

ACKNOWLEDGMENTS

I am deeply indebted to the fine publications that have made space for these poems:

Bennington Review: "Shrift"

Blunderbuss Magazine: "In Consideration of My Best Efforts" and "Viscosity"

Boog City Reader: "Samo for the So-Called Avant Garde," "Season of Inversion," "My Throat Incarnate," and "Justification in Reverse"

Boston Review: "Traveling Altar Bearing the Eight Auspicious Gestures"

Cartographer: "A Name"

The Cincinnati Review: "The Conditions of Reason"

Denver Quarterly: "(Mysterious and Subtle Mirror!)," "The First Gilt," and "Matthew"

Gettysburg Review: "Ask"

Gulf Stream Magazine: "A Knife at the Crossroads, Pointing East"

Horsethief: "The Other Trodden in Clover and Timothy"

The Iowa Review: "Facing the Water," "Analgesia," "Question," "Self Portrait with Lacrimae Rerum and Eyelid Pulled Down," "Never and Beast," "River," "Calve," and "Of the Hermit Bent Double by His Chains and His Follower"

The Iowa Review Online: "Genuflection"

The Journal: "The Ecstatic Limit of the Thou Art That"

Lana Turner: "Heaven's Gate" and "During the Meteor Shower"

Phantom Limb: "Dendrite"

Poetry Northwest: "To Shrike" and "Never Do Housework with Imperfect Intent"

Small Orange: "Public Works"

"Never Do Housework with Imperfect Intent" was selected by Natalie Diaz for inclusion in the anthology *Best New Poets 2017* (Samovar Press/Meridian).

"When You Tell Me No Bird" was published in an earlier form as part of a celebration of sonnets constructed with found text organized by the Folger Shakespeare Library and the 92nd Street Y.

A clutch of these poems appears in the chapbook *Lucid Animal*, which won the *Harbor Review* Editor's Prize. I am deeply grateful to the editors at *Harbor Review* for their careful attention.

Support from the 92nd Street Y's Discovery Contest, the Catwalk Institute, and the Columbia University School of the Arts Dean's Travel Grant was foundational to the research behind much of this work.

Thank you to everyone at *Burnside Review*, particularly Sid Miller and Dan Kaplan, for believing in this book. I'm so honored to be in the company of the authors you've published.

Thank you to my mentors and teachers, particularly Mark
Bibbins, Rivka Galchen, Margaret Gibson, Alan Gilbert, Donna
Hollenberg, Eleanor Johnson, Binnie Kirschenbaum, Dorothea
Lasky, Marilyn Nelson, V. Penelope Pelizzon, Alice Quinn, Ariana
Reines, Bill Wadsworth, Brenda Wineapple, and Alan Ziegler.

Thank you, Richard Howard—I'm forever astonished that you
held and cared for these poems, that you opened the window of
my mind in the window of yours. Thank you, Timothy Donnelly,
for knowing where I'm from and where I am. Thank you to the
incomparable and incandescent (even and especially now) Lucie
Brock-Broido, without whom not.

Thank you to my fellow students and readers at Columbia,
particularly my thesis cohort: L.A. Johnson, Shane Manieri,
Elizabeth Metzger, Richard Quigley, and Kay Zhang—you had these
poems in the middle of the night. Thank you, Carlie Hoffman,
for believing in this book and for taking so much time with it.
Thank you, Matt Alston, Elise Brandenberg, Michelle Craig,
Eric Danton, Carolina Ebeid, Regan Good, Melissa Green,
Shandra Green, Matthea Harvey, Andrea Henchey, Ricardo
Alberto Maldonado, Melissa Mullins, Abby Ohlheiser, Max Ritvo,
Christina Rumpf, Arthur Seefahrt, Carla Stockton, Mika Taylor,
Gwyneth Troyer, and Jasmine Dreame Wagner.

Jennifer Chang, I will never feel sure I have found the right way
to thank you for seeing in this book what you saw. Your poems are
cardinal. You've helped me find my place in the landscape.

Thank you to my family. My brother, Patrick, and my sister, Nora—
we know where we're from. Thank you to my children, Rory,
Vivian, and Éamon, for being such good sports about having a poet
mom. Rory, that thing you said about the motion of flocks and the
motion of my poems—I think about that more than you know.

Thank you, my Matthew Carey Salyer. I would not have any of this without you. You are my fiercest, most loyal supporter, my harshest (ha!) first reader, my right-hand man, my bouncer, my coach, my confidante. Your ear for poetry is unmatched and it has made me immeasurably better as a poet, just as your willingness to make this life with me has made me better as a human.

Most of all, thank you to my parents, Robert and Elizabeth Dahn. You made such a beautiful life for me. You taught me how to live with a landscape and be attentive to its minutia, that I was part of it, not merely in it. You let me read whatever I wanted to. You gave me the space to figure out who I was and never made me feel as though I was anything other than absolutely loved. This book is for you. You made a book of poems when you made me. And more.

Meghan Maguire Dahn grew up in the middle of the woods. Her first book, *Domain*, was selected by Jennifer Chang as the winner of the 2020 Burnside Review Press Book Award. She is also the author of the chapbook *Lucid Animal* (winner of the 2021 *Harbor Review* Editor's Prize). Her work has appeared in *Boston Review*, *The Iowa Review*, *Cincinnati Review*, *Denver Quarterly*, *Bennington Review*, and the anthology *Best New Poets 2017*. A winner of the 92nd Street Y's Discovery Contest in 2014, she has an MFA from Columbia University's School of the Arts and lives in New York City with her family.